International Labour Office

ASSISTING DISABLED PERSONS

IN FINDING EMPLOYMENT

A practical guide

Robert Heron
and
Barbara Murray

ILO East Asia Multidisciplinary Advisory Team
ILO Regional Office for Asia and the Pacific
Bangkok

First published 1997
Second Edition 2003

ISBN 92-2-115116-6

Printed in Uruguay

Foreword

Since this guide was first printed in Bangkok, Thailand, in 1997, in the context of the Asian and Pacific Decade of Disabled Persons, there has been an increasing emphasis globally on the need for ob placement services to pay specific attention to job-seekers with disabilities and to ensure that job placement personnel are adequately equipped to provide an effective service to this group of service users. The International Labour Office has received requests for technical advice and support, not only from countries of the Asian and Pacific Region, but also other regions of the world. In response to these requests, the guide has been translated into different national languages, including Arabic, Chinese, French, Khmer, Spanish, Thai and Vietnamese and customized to reflect the situation of people with disabilities in different regions.

This practical guide is part of the ILO's strategy to promote the observance of the ILO Vocational Rehabilitation and Employment (Disabled Persons) Convention, 1983 (No. 159), and Recommendation, 1983 (No. 168) and complement other ILO publications like the Code of Practice on Managing Disability in the Workplace.

The guide provides an overview of approaches and strategies to improve job opportunities for disabled jobseekers. It is intended for vocational guidance and placement personnel in mainstream and specialist employment services in governmental and non-governmental organizations. It will be of use to personnel providing such services to disabled people for some time, as well as those new to these tasks. It is also meant for policy-makers in labour administration.

The publication was developed for use in Asia by Barbara Murray, Senior Specialist in Vocational Rehabilitation, and Robert Heron, former Senior Labour Administration Specialist, with contributions by ILO consultants, Irene Gross Herzog and Maureen Gilbert.

The ILO is pleased to publish the second edition of this guide and hopes that, in combination with the customized guide for policy-makers and placement service managers "*Placement of Job-Seekers with Disabilities. Elements of an Effective Service*", and the ILO Resource Book for trainers of placement officers, it will continue contribute to the improvement of decent work opportunities for people with disabilities throughout the region.

Girma Agune
Director a.i.
Skills Department
ILO Geneva
October 2003

Table of contents

Foreword

1. People with disabilities: A diverse group   1

     A. General   1

     B. Barriers to employment   2

2. Disabled persons and employment   5

     A. Why is employment for disabled persons important?   5

     B. What are the problems disabled jobseekers face in finding work?   7

3. The placement officer's role   17

     A. Identifying work and jobs for disabled persons   18

     B. Overcoming obstacles   21

     C. Contacting employers   21

     D. Advising on legal requirements and financial assistance   22

     E. Building linkages   22

     F. What is expected of a placement officer?   22

4. Steps in assisting the job search   25

    A. Interviewing the jobseeker   25

    B. Recording information   29

    C. Identifying suitable jobs   30

    D. Matching the jobseeker and the job   33

5. Cooperating with employers   35

    A. Local labour market trends   36

    B. Convincing employers   36

    C. Changes to the workplace and work processes   39

    D. After placement   40

6. Getting started   43

1

People with disabilities: A diverse group

A. General

People with disabilities have much in common with non-disabled persons. They include women and men of all ages, living in urban and rural settings, with different personalities, abilities, aspirations and desires. They also differ significantly in their service needs.

The type of job for which a disabled person is suited may be influenced by whether he or she has an intellectual disability, a physical disability, a sensory disability, a mental health difficulty, or a combination of these. But this is less important than his or her knowledge, skills and general abilities when it comes to performing a job.

The ability of disabled persons to work - whether the disability is from birth or acquired later in life - is closely related to the extent to which they have come to terms with the disability and are able to live independently.

B. Barriers to employment

Work is central to the well-being of people with disabilities. But they face obstacles in finding and holding jobs. These obstacles may be:

- directly linked to their disability

- related to the environment in their communities and neighbourhoods.

> **The barriers which exclude disabled persons from employment-related services and opportunities are social, economic, cultural and political. All are real but all can be overcome.**

The obstacles they face include:

- negative attitudes, often linked to discrimination

- unequal access to education and training

- inaccessible buildings

- lack of accessible information

- inaccessible transport

- lack of assistive devices and support services

- low self-esteem and overprotective families

- lack of a supportive legal environment

- lack of policy support.

Although disabled persons may be unable to do certain things, with willingness and innovation the obstacles to meaningful employment are surmountable.

As job placement officer you must be aware of the barriers disabled persons face. Equally important, you must be prepared to help disabled persons find workable solutions to overcome these barriers. The main focus of your effort should be potential employers.

2

Disabled persons and employment

A. Why is employment for disabled persons important?

It is frequently assumed that persons with disabilities cannot or do not want to work. This is incorrect - disabled persons, like non-disabled persons, want to work and, given the **opportunity**, can and do work.

Disabled persons want and need to work to:

- earn a livelihood

- enjoy social contacts

- gain self-esteem.

Earning a livelihood

Work provides income to disabled persons to meet their basic needs.

Work provides the means to meet the additional costs associated with having a disability.

People with disabilities tell how getting a job changed their lives; those without a job talk of misery and despair.

> "Before I had a job I used to depend on others to get the things I needed. Now I am able to help my parents and sisters. I was also able to marry."
>
> Disabled worker
> Sri Lanka

> "Not having a job has led to financial difficulties and severe mental distress."
>
> Disabled jobseeker
> Sri Lanka

Social contact

Disabled persons have limited opportunities to meet people. Work provides such opportunities.

People with disabilities find that having a job reduces frustration and loneliness. Not having a job reinforces social isolation.

> "Having a job made a difference to my whole life. I was able to marry and have a family, and my attitude to others became more positive."
>
> Disabled worker
> Republic of Korea

> "Not having a job means having to do without some of the essentials you need and having to compromise on your self-respect when somebody else offers to buy them for you."
>
> Disabled jobseeker
> Sri Lanka

Self-esteem

Work, particularly paid employment, provides disabled persons with an opportunity to show they can contribute.

People with disabilities tell how work builds positive attitudes. Those without jobs lack pride and confidence in their own ability.

<table>
<tr>
<td>

"Having a job makes me feel more confident in myself and capable of contributing something to the society."

Disabled worker
Sri Lanka

</td>
<td>

"Without a job I felt gloomy, depressed and unfairly treated."

Disabled worker
Republic of Korea

</td>
</tr>
</table>

B. What are the problems disabled jobseekers face in finding work?

The main problems disabled persons face in their desire to work are:

- lack of education

- lack of employable skills

- rapidly changing labour markets

- employers' attitudes and perceptions

- lack of access to self-employment opportunities

- unfair terms of employment

- higher work-related costs.

In addition, disabled women and girls face a number of special problems.

Lack of education

Many disabled persons live in rural areas where isolation means a scarcity or absence of educational services.

Children with disabilities in isolated areas often remain uneducated due to prejudice, misunderstanding and the lack of special schools.

All children in isolated areas suffer from the limited resources available for education: disabled children suffer more because the resources are channelled to non-disabled children.

Even in urban areas, disabled children, depending on the type of disability, have limited educational opportunities.

> **In south Asia, 57 per cent of children complete five years of schooling.**
>
> **In east Asia and the Pacific, 85 per cent of children complete five years of schooling.**
>
> **In the Asian and Pacific region, as a whole, only about 5 per cent of children with disabilities attend school.**

The education completed by disabled children may not be recognized by certifying bodies. Such bodies may not accept the adjustments made to courses to allow disabled children to complete them.

This lack of recognition deprives many disabled individuals of **access to generally recognized certificates** and restricts their **access to vocational training** and related job opportunities.

Lack of employable skills

People with disabilities who participate in training courses may not receive recognized certificates.

> "I can't get a job because I have no proper vocational training or higher education."
>
> Disabled jobseeker
> Sri Lanka

Disabled persons, like non-disabled persons, may find the training they receive is not geared to job opportunities in the local area.

The lack of recognized skills or the acquisition of skills unrelated to labour market opportunities may result in no jobs or jobs that are routine, monotonous, low level, insecure and with no prospects.

> **Training courses should be adapted to the needs of disabled persons, not with a view to lowering standards but simply to accommodate their disability.**

Rapidly changing labour markets

Competitive pressure encourages the introduction of new technology. This, in turn, affects the structure of employment. Simple, labour-intensive tasks are eliminated and opportunities become available for workers with adaptable, multiple, higher-level skills.

Competition for jobs becomes more intense. Disabled persons, already disadvantaged due to the non-recognition of their qualifications, are at an even greater disadvantage as jobs previously available to them progressively disappear.

> **The structure of employment is changing. Disabled persons with low-level or redundant skills will find it even more difficult to secure jobs.**

Technological change has positive aspects too.

- Telework offers some people with mobility impairments the possibility of working from home, thereby reducing problems of accessibility, transport and fatigue.

- Information technology provides an opportunity for disabled persons, who have difficulty in attending training centres, to learn at home.

- Improved assistive devices are becoming available with technological advances. These devices can help disabled persons' employment prospects. They include special computer software, adapted cars and equipment, and lightweight wheelchairs.

> **New devices still depend on suitable environmental conditions. For example, no matter how innovative the design and construction of a wheelchair may be, it still requires low kerbs, wide doorways, and elevators.**

Employer attitudes and perceptions

Employers frequently regard disabled persons as unsuitable for employment.

> "It is difficult to get a job because disabled persons are considered to be invalids."
>
> "It was difficult to convince the employer that it **is** possible to travel and work using a wheelchair."
>
> Disabled jobseekers
> Sri Lanka

Changing employer attitudes can be a slow process. It is necessary to provide employers with new information and the opportunity to discuss and reflect on the employment of disabled people.

The placement officer has a role to play.

- Inform potential employers about success stories of disabled workers.

- Persuade employers to see for themselves through work trials for disabled persons.

- Convince employers that disabled workers can be productive, reliable and loyal.

The placement officer may need to examine his or her own attitudes towards disabled persons, too.

Lack of access to self-employment opportunities

All persons seeking to commence their own business need advisory services, training, and access to credit and markets.

But disabled persons may need additional assistance to adapt their equipment and workplace to their particular needs.

> Examples:
>
> Changing bench heights at the workstation.
>
> Purchasing adapted software for a self-employed computer operator.

Self-employed people with disabilities may need extra subsidies and grants for these adaptations.

Unfair terms of employment

Once employed, disabled persons may have no formal contract of employment and may not receive their full entitlements (e.g. the minimum wage).

Employment security for disabled workers is often less than for non-disabled workers: they may be the first to lose their jobs in the event of lay-offs.

In some cases there is no special legal protection for disabled persons. There may be situations in which disabled persons are **prevented by law from entering into contracts.**

Higher work-related costs

Although having a job provides real benefits for disabled persons, they often face higher costs related to working.

> Examples:
>
> Wheelchair users frequently have to travel by taxi rather than cheaper public transport.
>
> Disabled persons may need to purchase higher, more expensive wheelchairs for greater mobility in going to work and at work itself.
>
> Disabled persons often have to meet the work-related costs of wear and tear on appliances, clothing and footwear.

Special problems for disabled women and girls

Although opportunities for women in education are improving and attitudes towards their education and training are more positive, little has changed for women with disabilities. Job opportunities for disabled women continue to be rare.

Disabled women face greater discrimination than women in general. Together with limited skills, and in some circumstances limited mobility, this often means that homework is the only available employment opportunity for many disabled women.

Homework may involve long hours, unsafe raw materials and unreasonably low piece-work rates.

> **Overall, disabled women receive less pay than disabled men, and less pay than non-disabled women.**

Because of their vulnerability, disabled women workers may face greater possibilities of sexual harassment than other women.

3 | The placement officer's role

The placement officer has two major roles:

- helping jobseekers find suitable employment

- helping enterprises find suitable staff.

The roles apply to the placement of disabled and non-disabled persons, but for disabled persons additional tasks are involved:

- identifying work and jobs disabled persons can do

- finding ways to overcome the obstacles disabled persons face in seeking and securing employment

- contacting employers and convincing them to employ disabled workers

- advising employers on legal requirements, and both employers and disabled persons on financial assistance

- building linkages with other agencies and organizations concerned.

A. Identifying work and jobs
for disabled persons

As placement officer you can identify work and jobs for disabled persons in
four main ways.

- Start with a disabled jobseeker, and then search for a job that matches his or her abilities and requirements.

- Start with the requirements of an available job, and then search for a suitable disabled person to fill it.

- Start with the legal requirement that the employer must fill a quota for disabled persons, and then see what work disabled persons can do in that enterprise.

- Start with an employer who expresses willingness to employ disabled persons, but without any particular jobs in mind, and then see what work would be suitable for disabled persons.

> **Rarely are disabled persons the "perfect" candidates for job vacancies. Strive for the best possible match between the work to be performed and the skills, abilities and requirements of disabled jobseekers.**

As placement officer you need to consider your approach to interviewing jobseekers.

- Listen carefully.

- Give the disabled jobseeker time to express himself or herself.

- Encourage the disabled jobseeker to decide for himself or herself.

- Talk directly to the disabled person, not to helpers or friends who may be present.

- Use body language that is supportive.

(Interviewing is dealt with in more detail in Chapter 4.)

As placement officer you should not adopt rigid ideas concerning the kinds of work disabled persons can do.

- Many disabled persons can do a wide range of work.

- Do not assume disabled persons can do only simple manual and routine work (such as packing and sorting).

- For many jobs a disability is no obstacle at all to full and effective performance.

- A disability is only **one aspect** of a person's make-up - personality, motivation, training and natural talents are more important.

As placement officer you need to consider the work to be performed, and also be aware of the environment in which it will take place.

> **It is normally assumed that deaf persons cannot do a job where using a telephone is essential. But special telephone devices for deaf persons and the increasing use of electronic mail can change the working environment and make it possible for them to do such work.**

As placement officer you should find out about working conditions (e.g. wages, hours of work, shift arrangements, overtime) and the degree of flexibility for a particular job (e.g. starting and finishing times).

As placement officer you need to think beyond **job analysis** to the wider issue of **work analysis**. (This is considered in Chapter 4.)

As placement officer you should be aware of the physical layout of the premises in which work will take place and relate this to the person's disability.

Example:

Staircases, narrow doorways and a lack of ramps or elevators will make it difficult to place wheelchair users in jobs at such places. But it may be possible for the premises to be adapted or the job to be located on the ground floor.

B. Overcoming obstacles

As placement officer you are in a position to address some of the obstacles disabled persons face in finding work.

In particular, you are able to influence the negative attitudes of employers. (This is dealt with in Chapter 5.)

Changing employer attitudes may involve changing your own attitudes first.

C. Contacting employers

As placement officer your task is to convince the employer to create a new job specifically for a disabled person, modify an existing job to suit a disabled person, give a disabled person the opportunity to work in an unmodified job or offer a work trial to a disabled person.

Find out as much as possible about the enterprise and its policy before the initial meeting.

Start by providing information, discussing, negotiating and persuading.

Once the employer agrees on a placement, discuss and negotiate the job description and employment conditions and, if necessary, workplace changes.

Try to ensure that the **first placement** is a success. This may lead to more placements.

D. Advising on legal requirements and financial assistance

As placement officer you may be required to provide information to employers on quotas, grants and financial incentives for employing disabled persons:

- wage subsidies
- tax concessions
- workplace adaptation grants
- preferential treatment.

E. Building linkages

As placement officer you are able to build linkages between:

- the disabled person and prospective employer

- the disabled person and community organizations and agencies willing and able to assist (disabled persons' organizations, trade unions, employers' organizations, vocational training institutions).

F. What is expected of a placement officer?

A placement officer needs to be aware of what disabled persons and employers expect of him or her.

What do disabled persons expect?

Help in finding work that meets disabled persons' abilities and personal requirements (e.g. location, hours of work).

- Advice on how long it will take to find work.

- Information on specific job vacancies and their locations.

- Information about training opportunities.

- Advice on the requirements of specific jobs in which they may be interested.

- Advice on drafting job application letters and on preparing for job interviews that disabled persons have found on their own initiative.

- Information on work-experience programmes and work-trial opportunities.

- Assurance that disabled persons will be kept informed of progress in finding work.

- Reassurance concerning disabled persons' suitability for work, in general, or for a particular job.

- Assistance in encouraging employers to make workplace and workstation adaptations.

- ssistance in negotiating non-standard terms and conditions of employment.

- Follow-up after placement to assist in solving problems.

What do employers expect?

- Referral of disabled people able to do the job as specified or modified.

- Information on laws, quotas and financial assistance concerning the employment of disabled persons.

- Information on different forms of disability.

- Advice on the effect, on co-workers and supervisors, of employing persons with disabilities.

- Information and advice on safety and accessibility for disabled workers.

- Advice on adaptations to workplaces and workstations.

- Assurance that you are available to provide follow-up support and respond to problems.

> **As placement officer you can help disabled jobseekers in their own job searches or actively represent them and negotiate with employers on their behalf.**

Steps in assisting in the job search

The basic steps in assisting a disabled person in finding employment are:

- interviewing the jobseeker

- recording information

- identifying a suitable job

- matching the jobseeker and the job.

A. Interviewing the jobseeker

Interviewing is a process of interaction between the placement officer and the disabled jobseeker. The aim is to obtain information as a basis for making decisions.

Information should be obtained on:

- general particulars (name, age, address, telephone)

- educational level

- vocational qualifications

- acquired skills

- work experience

- job expectations concerning working conditions (e.g. working hours, wages)

- support available from family

- nature of disability

- general mobility

- interests and aspirations

- needs related to the disability (e.g. ramps, elevators, personal assistance).

In conducting the interview the placement officer should:

- help the disabled person feel comfortable and relaxed

- allocate sufficient time to obtain information

- talk to the disabled person directly (not through assistants or advocates)

- use body language that supports words and intentions

- listen attentively to answers to questions

- concentrate on obtaining facts.

The success of an interview will depend on how the placement officer interacts with the disabled jobseeker. The outcome will depend on the placement officer's ability to talk, listen and observe.

The interview consists of three main parts:

- the beginning

- the middle

- the end.

In the **beginning**, the placement officer establishes rapport and makes clear the purpose of the interview.

In the **middle**, the placement officer concentrates on obtaining information which will assist in finding a job for the disabled person.

The interview will **end** when the placement officer has obtained all the required information or when the time available is over.

The interview process involves the skills of:

- talking

- listening

- observing.

Talking involves asking questions and giving explanations. Your questions may be 'closed', requiring specific answers, or 'open', seeking general information and longer responses.

In asking questions:

- avoid technical and complicated language

- avoid long questions

- avoid multiple questions

- avoid long statements.

Listening requires concentration and patience, and body language that shows you are interested in what the interviewee is saying.

Observing can assist in clarifying what you hear by being conscious of hand and body movements, facial expressions and posture.

B. Recording information

As placement officer you will need to record information about:

- jobseekers

- enterprises

- job vacancies.

Information on **disabled jobseekers** can be recorded on cards or on computer. This is the process of **registration**.

- Keep the registration process as simple as possible.

- Encourage re-registration at regular intervals by telephone or letter.

- Encourage disabled jobseekers to let you know if they find jobs through their own efforts.

Information on **enterprises** should cover:

- general information (including name, address, contact details)

- specific information relevant to the placement of disabled workers:

  - disabled persons currently employed and their jobs

  - possibility for work-experience and work-trial programmes

  - suitability of locations, premises and workstations for disabled persons.

Information on **job vacancies** should cover:

- descriptions of job vacancies (preferably with a national classification code)

- vacancies suitable for disabled persons.

C. Identifying suitable jobs

As placement officer you need to know about the content of jobs. This will help you to decide:

- the suitability of a disabled person for a job

- the suitability of a job for a disabled person

- the adaptations required to enable a disabled person to do the job.

Identifying suitable jobs requires the ability to undertake:

- work analysis

- job analysis.

Work analysis involves examining the work process, as a whole, to determine whether a new job suitable for a disabled person could be created if the work were reorganized.

> **In an office the work of photocopying, collating and binding documents is piling up and staff are too busy with other tasks. This provides an opportunity to advise the employer to create a new job to enable a disabled person to do all the photocopying and related work.**

Work analysis enables the placement officer to identify elements of existing jobs which could be combined into a new job. Jobs identified in this way tend to be routine and repetitive, but provide the disabled person with an opportunity which may lead to a better job in future.

Work analysis provides the placement officer with an opportunity to see whether a job might be created that suits the needs of part-time or temporary disabled workers; it also offers the possibility of work-experience programmes.

Job analysis involves finding out:

- what a worker does

- how the work is done

- where the work is done

- the skills and abilities required to do the work

- the conditions under which the work is done.

Job analysis entails:

- **observing** the work being done in the enterprise as a whole

- **observing** the work being done in a particular job

- **interviewing** workers, supervisors and personnel managers

- **listening** to workers, other disabled persons, supervisors and managers.

> **Jobs are more complex than they look. As placement officer you should observe workers doing the actual job, interview other people and, if possible, perform some of the tasks yourself. In doing so, relate the tasks to the impairment of the disabled person.**

D. Matching the jobseeker and the job

The matching of the jobseeker and the job is a key task for the placement officer.

It is not always possible to make a perfect match and compromises may need to be made if the disabled jobseeker:

- lacks work experience

- lacks training.

Where a disabled jobseeker lacks experience and training, it may be possible to convince the employer to give the person a work trial which will provide an opportunity to acquire experience and skills.

Job matching is made difficult where the employer has unrealistically high expectations concerning the qualifications for a particular job.

> An employer may require the completion of secondary education for a relatively simple job such as chair caning. As placement officer you should try to convince the employer that disabled jobseekers on your register could do the job even though they don't have the educational level specified.

5 | Cooperating with employers

Without the employer there will be no work or jobs for disabled persons. As placement officer your task is to convince the employer to meet his or her need for qualified workers by recruiting suitable disabled jobseekers. This can be done by:

- offering an unmodified job

- modifying an existing job

- creating a new job.

Your contact with the employer falls into three main categories:

- finding out as much as possible about the world of work and labour market trends in your locality

- convincing employers to engage disabled persons by providing information, and through discussion, negotiation and persuasion

- discussing and negotiating changes to the workplace, job descriptions and conditions of employment once the employer agrees on placement.

A. Local labour market trends

Visiting enterprises regularly broadens the placement officer's knowledge about the world of work in the area under his or her jurisdiction.

You should find out:

- which enterprises are growing or contracting, and what jobs are involved

- what technological changes are taking place, and how these will affect jobs.

B. Convincing employers

As placement officer you should find out about the enterprise's policy and attitude to the employment of disabled persons. Make every effort to assess the corporate culture.

> **If the corporate culture is highly profit oriented, your contact with the employer will focus on the economic aspects of employing disabled persons (e.g. the availability of financial incentives, labour productivity). If the corporate culture is more socially oriented, you should focus on securing work trials for disabled persons.**

Encourage the employer to consider employing disabled persons by providing information on success stories from other enterprises.

The employer may be willing to consider employing disabled persons but may not know which work may be suitable. You should use your work analysis and job analysis skills to identify work possibilities and advise the employer.

If the employer shows interest in employing disabled persons, find out:

- which work areas are suitable for persons with mobility difficulties

- whether transport to and from work is provided

- whether disabled persons are employed at present

- whether the employer is prepared to provide structured work trials

- whether training opportunities are available

- whether apprenticeship training includes disabled persons.

Plan your visit to each enterprise. Make an appointment and find out as much as possible about the enterprise before your visit.

When you visit the enterprise:

- be punctual

- indicate clearly the purpose of the visit

- provide accurate information

- be concise - don't make speeches

- bring relevant printed information

- observe actual work situations, if possible.

> **Stress that you are providing a service, not seeking charity. Look at it from an employer's viewpoint.**

If the employer is receptive to employing disabled persons, collect details of possible jobs:

- number of jobs

- job descriptions

- working hours

- working environment

- terms and conditions of employment

- availability of transport

- availability of training.

Examine job descriptions to assess the functional literacy and numeracy requirements of each job. If the required education levels appear unrealistically high, discuss this with the employer.

> **If the employer has not employed disabled persons before, do everything possible to make the first placement successful. A positive experience may persuade the employer to engage more disabled persons in future.**

C. Changes to the workplace and work processes

Discussions on adapting the workplace and work processes should take place **after** securing placement.

In most cases, disabled persons can be placed without major changes to the workplace and work routines.

Adaptation, if required, may take various forms:

- changes in the physical layout of the enterprise (e.g. wider doorways, wider passageways, ramps)

- changes to the workstation (e.g. adjusting bench heights, providing brighter lighting)

- the purchase of special equipment to assist disabled workers

- changes to work procedures and the reallocation of work between staff.

> **Where employers are reluctant to make workplace adaptations, they may be persuaded to do so by the availability of subsidies.**

> **Employers should be advised that adaptations are not necessarily expensive and often are not required at all. Adaptations could be beneficial to all workers, not only to those with disabilities.**

Adaptations may include changes additional to those within the workplace:

- arranging accommodation nearer to the enterprise

- arranging for a personal assistant to give support

- arranging for colleagues to assist where necessary.

D. After placement

Cooperating with employers also involves you in providing follow-up to the placement process which can assist:

- you, as placement officer

- the disabled worker

- the employer.

Follow-up can assist **you** in:

- identifying any stress and anxiety experienced by the disabled worker in the early stages of the job

- identifying whether the disabled worker can actually **do** the job

- seeing whether additional workstation adaptations are necessary

- demonstrating to the disabled worker and the employer that you are interested and concerned

- evaluating the quality of your job-matching process

- determining how well training institutions prepare disabled persons for actual work situations

- providing feedback to the agencies concerned.

Follow-up can assist **the disabled worker** in keeping the job if you ask such questions as:

- How are you getting on in the job?

- Do you think you will stay on after the probation period?

- Is your job still the same?

- How many hours do you work?

- Are the employment conditions and salary as promised?

- Are you having any particular problems?

- What adjustments have been made to your workstation?

Follow-up can assist **the employer** by focusing attention on the disabled worker and the job with a view to minimizing problems. Ask the employer:

- Are you happy with the worker?

- Have your expectations been met?

- What is the worker's attitude to the job?

- How does the worker relate to fellow workers?

- How do fellow workers relate to the disabled worker?

- What problems does the worker have?

- Do you intend to retain the worker after the probation period?

During the follow-up visit you should take the opportunity to find out whether the employer is interested in employing other disabled workers. If the employer is interested, obtain details of possible jobs. If the employer is reluctant, find out why.

> **Follow-up can be demanding on your time and it will not be possible to follow up every placement. Priority should be given to disabled persons in their first job, disabled persons undergoing on-the-job training and disabled persons requiring ongoing support.**

6

Getting started

As placement officer you play an important role in helping disabled persons find work. This requires you to understand the difficulties disabled people face and, more importantly, to do something positive to overcome or reduce the difficulties.

Be aware

People with disabilities are excluded from mainstream society and employment by a number of barriers:

- negative attitudes
- lack of access to education and training
- inaccessible buildings
- lack of accessible information
- inaccessible transport
- lack of assistive devices and support services
- low self-esteem and overprotective families
- lack of a supportive legal environment
- lack of supportive policies.

> **Many disabled persons have never had a job; other disabled persons work for short periods with no job security. The reasons for this relate more to how work is organized and employer attitudes than to their disability.**

Attitudes are central

Negative attitudes are the most widespread barrier disabled persons face, and sometimes lead to discrimination.

> **Negative stereotypes about disabled persons (frequently false) result in limited opportunities to do the things they would like to do - have a job, have a home of their own, marry, have children.**

Education and training are essential

The lack of education and training opportunities seriously affects the employment prospects of disabled persons.

> "I can't get a job because I have no proper vocational training or higher education."
>
> Disabled jobseeker
> Sri Lanka

Access to buildings is important

Access to buildings and mobility within buildings, especially workplaces, are major problems for many disabled persons, particularly wheelchair users, individuals with visual impairments and people with other mobility difficulties.

Improved access to buildings and other modifications need not be expensive and can benefit everyone, not only workers with disabilities.

Information is vital

Information is a vital part of the process of helping disabled people secure employment. This includes information:

- for the disabled persons themselves

- for those providing employment services to disabled persons

- for employers and potential employers

- for co-workers.

> **Information for people with disabilities should be in a format sensitive to the nature of their disability.**

> **Information for non-disabled people should include general information about different forms of disability, as well as on the rights and obligations of employers who engage disabled persons.**

Getting to and from work is fundamental

Workers with disabilities frequently face difficulties in commuting to work. The difficulties can be overcome by arranging for:

- subsidized or free transport

- specially adapted vehicles

- assistants to travel with them.

> **Assistance in commuting can be arranged, but is frequently beyond the means of the disabled worker. The employment service may be able to provide direct assistance or arrange it through employers or community-support groups.**

Disabled persons may need reassurance

Faced with negative attitudes and barriers of exclusion, some disabled persons come to believe the negative stereotypes of themselves. As a result, disabled persons have low self-confidence, and do not believe in their ability to take charge of their own lives.

> **Reassurance can be provided through peer-support groups in which disabled persons can learn from each other and from people with disabilities who have been successful in securing jobs.**

What can you do?

As placement officer you can assist disabled persons by:

- understanding their feelings and expectations

- providing employment opportunities.

Understanding disabled persons requires that you accept:

- they are people first - the disability is secondary

- individuals with disabilities are not all the same

- they have ambitions, like everybody

- disabled persons can make their own decisions

- they want to be consulted on matters affecting them.

Assisting disabled persons in finding and keeping jobs requires you to:

- listen to what they need

- reassure them about their abilities

- provide ongoing support, where required

- encourage the formation of peer-support groups

- raise the awareness of your colleagues and work contacts about the abilities and rights of disabled persons.

> **You can assist disabled persons in finding work.**
>
> **Make a start!**
>
> **Your assistance will make a difference.**

Printed in

CINTERFOR

Montevideo - Uruguay

D.L : 330.693/2003

www.ingramcontent.com/pod-product-compliance
Lightning Source LLC
Chambersburg PA
CBHW030030290326
41934CB00005B/565